Contents

In the beginning

To know what is inside the Earth, we need to look back at where our planet came from. Its story started 4600 million years ago.

Gas cloud

The star we call the Sun, and all the objects going around it, are together called the Solar System. These objects include the Earth and seven other planets, their moons and countless smaller lumps of rock. They all began as a vast cloud of gas and dust spinning in space.

The Sun and planets gradually formed from a giant whirling cloud in space.

Tell me more!

The dust and gas that became our Solar System probably formed when a huge, old star blew apart in an explosion called a **supernova**. Everything in the Solar System, therefore, is made of stardust – the Sun, the planets and their moons, and even us!

INSIDE EARTH

Series Editor: STEVE PARKER

DAVID AND HELEN ORME

QED Publishing

Designer and Picture Researcher Louise Downey
Project Editor Michael Downey

Copyright © QED Publishing 2010

First published in the UK in 2010 by
QED Publishing
A Quarto Group company
226 City Road
London EC1V 2TT

www.qed-publishing.co.uk

A catalogue record for this book is
available from the British Library.

ISBN 978 1 84835 480 7

Printed in China

Picture Credits

Key: t=top, b=bottom, c=centre,
FC=front cover

Corbis 11t Colin Garratt; Milepost 92$^{1/2}$/ 14-15
Julie Dermansky/ 27t Patrick Pleul-dpa
Louise Downey 15t
Getty Images 12-13 Philip and Karen Smith
NASA 4b ESA, J. Hester, A. Loll (ASU)/ 7t
Photoshot 18 NHPA/ 19b Woodfall Wild
Images/ 21 World Pictures/ 24 NHPA/ 25
Xinhua/ 26t Xinhua/ 29 NHPA/
Science Photo Library 4-5 Mark Garlick/
7 Mark Garlick/ 8t SPL/ 8b Lynette Cook/ 11b
Patrick Landmann/ 12b Gary Hincks/ 14b
Karim Agabi / Eurellios/ 18b Gary Hincks/ 20b
Gary Hinks/ 22b Javier Trueba / MSF/ 26b Gary
Hincks
Shutterstock 1/ 2-3/ 30-31/ 32 Chris Hill/
5b Linda Brotkorb/ 6 sdecoret/ 9t Galyna
Andrushko/ 10 argonaut/ 16 Nikki Bidgood /
17b Jose Gil/ 17 Vulkanette/ 19t Beschi/ 21c
Elena Elisseeva/ 22-23t Dmitri Melnik/ 22c Don
Bendickson/ 23b Jiri Vaclavek/ 25t Geowulf/
26-27 Tonylady/ 28 Pichugin Dmitry/ 29b
William Allum

Words in **bold** are
explained in the
Glossary on page 30.

Sun and planets

As the cloud whirled around, small amounts of gas and dust began to clump together. This happened because of the pulling power that all matter has, called gravity. Some clumps slowly became bigger and heavier. The largest, in the centre, formed the Sun and started to shine. Smaller clumps became the planets.

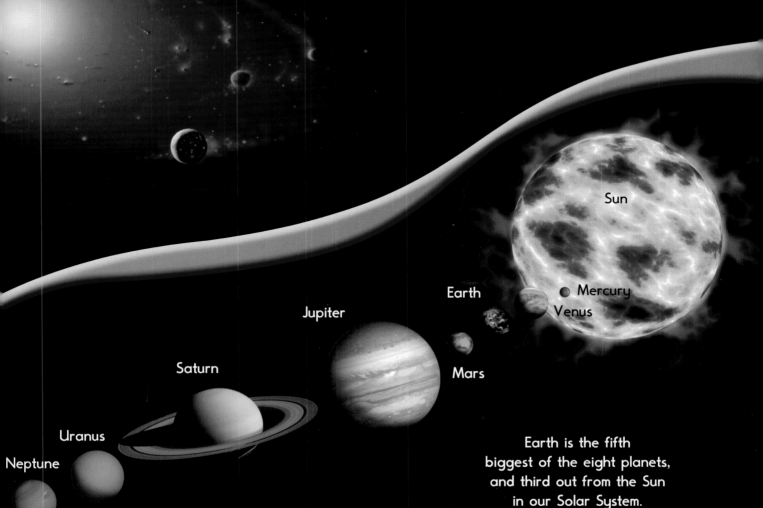

Sun

Mercury

Venus

Earth

Mars

Jupiter

Saturn

Uranus

Neptune

Earth is the fifth biggest of the eight planets, and third out from the Sun in our Solar System.

Early Earth

As gas and dust clumped together to form the Earth, they became extremely hot. Gradually, our planet took shape as a spinning ball.

Massive bang

Early in its history, it is possible that the Earth was hit by another, smaller planet. This collision may have knocked a chunk out of the Earth, which became the Moon. The collision may also have tilted the Earth, which does not spin upright, but slightly to one side.

A smaller planet may have crashed into the Earth not long after it formed.

Red-hot world

Slowly, parts of the Earth's surface began to harden into solid rock. Other parts of the surface remained as red-hot liquid rock. Huge volcanoes spurted out poison gases in many places. There was no life for a billion years.

Tell me more!

The gas and dust cloud that formed the Solar System was not the only one in space. Around the universe, billions of other clouds formed stars and planets in the same way. Many are being formed right now!

The surface of the early Earth was made up of boiling rocks and huge volcanoes.

Bringing water

During our Solar System's early history, there were millions of lumps of rock and ice hurtling around in space. Thousands of these smashed into the Earth. Some of these, called **comets**, may have brought water to Earth as it cooled.

Layered Earth

The Earth is made up of layers. These start with the inner core at the centre and end with the crust.

Earth's crust

The outer layer of the Earth is known as the crust. This is the layer we live on. In some places, such as at the bottom of the sea, the crust is only 5 kilometres thick. In other places, especially under mountains, the crust can be up to 60 kilometres thick.

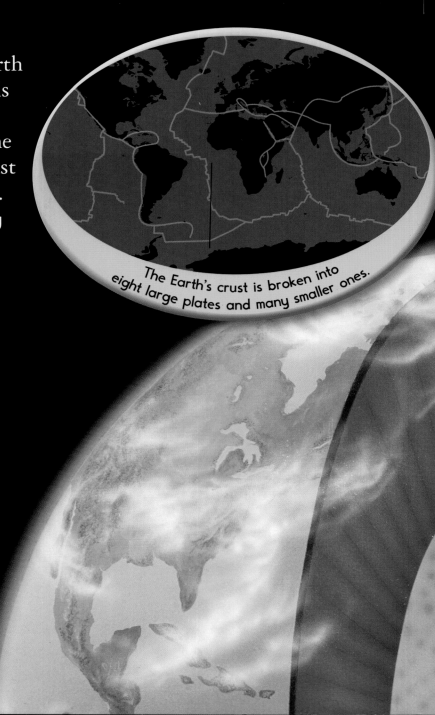

The Earth's crust is broken into eight large plates and many smaller ones.

Jagged edges

The Earth's crust is not one solid piece. It is more like a cracked eggshell around an egg. The crust is made of huge, curved pieces that have jagged edges. These fit together like the pieces of a gigantic jigsaw puzzle.

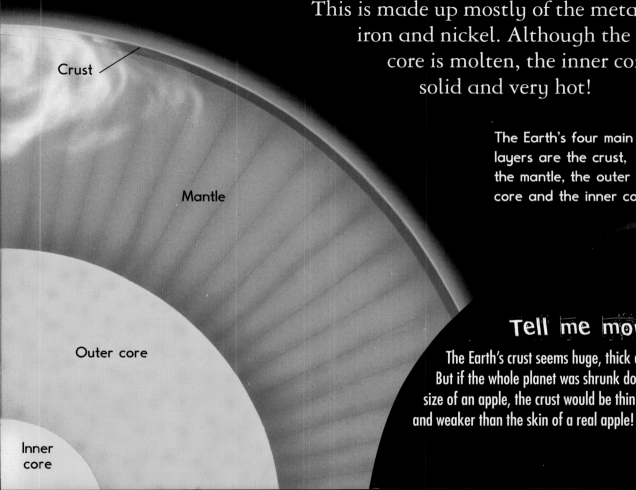

This is made up mostly of the metal iron and nickel. Although the core is molten, the inner core solid and very hot!

The Earth's four main layers are the crust, the mantle, the outer core and the inner co

Crust

Mantle

Outer core

Inner core

Tell me mo
The Earth's crust seems huge, thick
But if the whole planet was shrunk do
size of an apple, the crust would be thin
and weaker than the skin of a real apple!

Hot core

The Earth has been around for more than 4000 million years. Its crust is cool but its middle, or core, is still extremely hot. Can we work out how hot?

Hotter than the Sun

It is not possible for scientists to drill down to the inner core to measure how hot it is. Instead, they have to make complicated calculations. Scientists believe that at the centre of the Earth the temperature may be as high as 7000 degrees Celsius. This is hotter than the surface of the Sun!

The deepest that people have drilled into the crust is about 12 kilometres. This is less than one-third of the way through the crust.

Staying hot

Part of the heat that comes from the Earth's core is heat left over from when the Earth was first formed. Heat is also created in the core by **radioactive substances**. These give off large amounts of heat as they slowly break down into simpler substances. This is what happens in a nuclear power station. The radioactive fuel gives off heat, which is then used to generate electricity.

Tell me more!

How deep into the Earth can people go? There are gold mines in South Africa that are nearly 4 kilometres deep. Some of these mines are fitted with special equipment that keeps miners cool. Underground temperatures can reach a blistering 70 degrees Celsius!

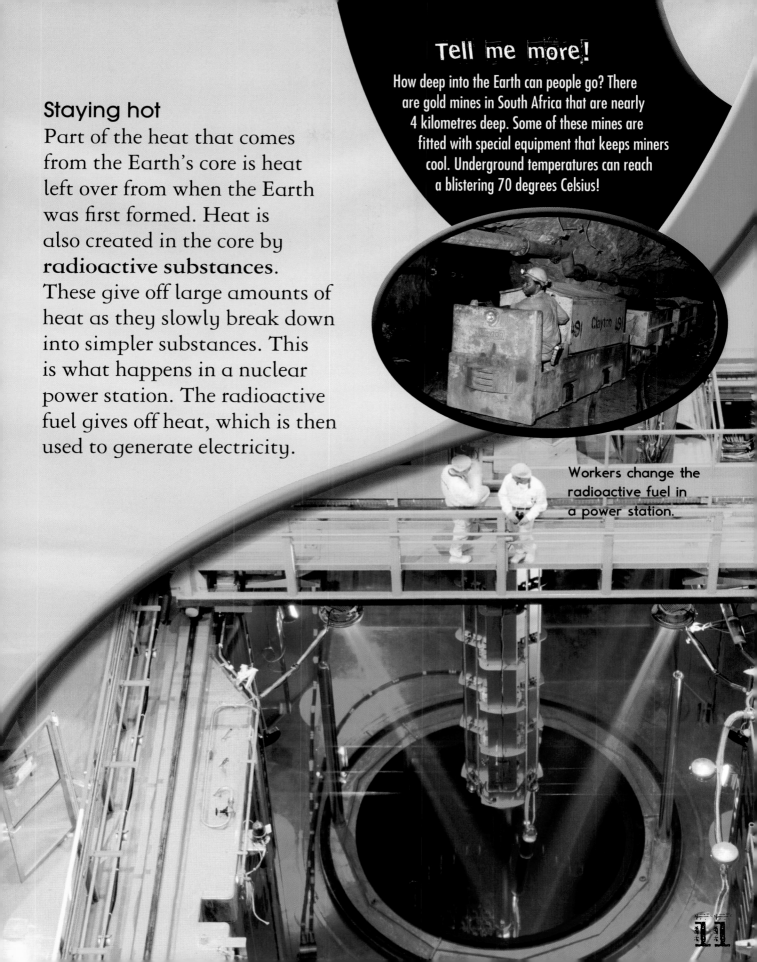

Workers change the radioactive fuel in a power station.

11

Earth's magnetism

Deep inside the Earth, the core is slowly moving and flowing in circles. How do we know this happens? We know this because of the magnetic **compass**!

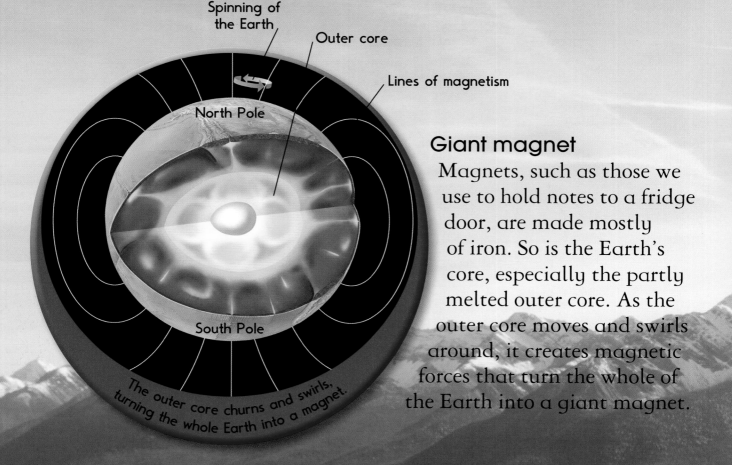

Spinning of the Earth

Outer core

Lines of magnetism

North Pole

South Pole

The outer core churns and swirls, turning the whole Earth into a magnet.

Giant magnet

Magnets, such as those we use to hold notes to a fridge door, are made mostly of iron. So is the Earth's core, especially the partly melted outer core. As the outer core moves and swirls around, it creates magnetic forces that turn the whole of the Earth into a giant magnet.

How a compass works

A compass needle is a long, thin magnet. When it can turn freely, it lines up with the magnetism of the whole Earth. The ends of the compass needle point to the places where Earth's magnetism is strongest – the North Pole at the top of the planet, and the South Pole at the bottom.

People can discover which way is north by using a compass.

Tell me more!

Every few million years, the Earth's magnetism reverses, or flips. The North Pole becomes the South Pole, and the other way around. In a few thousand years, this may happen again. Then, a compass needle's north end will point south!

13

The mantle

The mantle forms more than four-fifths of the whole Earth. It is so hot that some of its rocks are melted or molten.

During an earthquake, the ground can shake and move so much that buildings collapse. This happened in Haiti in 2010.

Moving mantle

The outer part of the mantle, at the bottom of the crust, has a temperature of about 500 degrees Celsius. The inner mantle, which is next to the core, is more than 4000 degrees Celsius. Rocks in the mantle slowly flow up, sideways and down again.

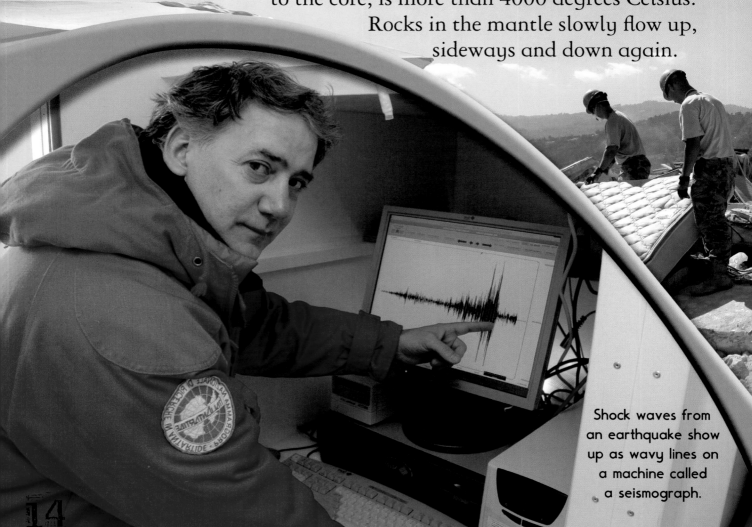

Shock waves from an earthquake show up as wavy lines on a machine called a seismograph.

Shock waves

An earthquake is the sudden jolting of the enormous crust plates as they rub past each other. This jolting sends out shock waves, also called seismic waves. Some waves travel through the crust. Others pass into the Earth and are bent by the mantle and core to reach the Earth's surface far away. The speed and extent of bending show us what the mantle is made of.

Crust

Mantle

Outer core

Inner core

Earthquake

Seismic waves bend as they pass through the Earth's mantle and core.

Tell me more!

Seismic waves, which travel between one and 15 kilometres per second, may take more than an hour to reach the opposite side of the world. By that time they are weak and only a seismograph can detect them.

Rocky crust

The rocks that form our planet are made in different ways.

Soft rocks have been worn away by wind and rain to leave these hard granite rocks.

Rock types

There are three basic rock types. These are the **igneous**, **sedimentary** and **metamorphic** rocks. Igneous rocks form when extremely hot and runny lava or magma cool down and become solid.

Tell me more!

The world's biggest single rock, 350 metres high and 9.5 kilometres around, is Uluru in Central Australia. It is made of the sedimentary rock sandstone.

Magma rocks

The molten rock deep in the Earth's crust and mantle is called magma. This runny rock can rise up nearer to the surface, cool and then harden into an igneous rock, such as granite. These rocks are seen when the surface of the Earth is worn away by wind and rain to uncover deeper layers.

Lava rocks

Magma can also rise up to the surface through a weak part in the Earth's crust. When this happens in volcanoes, the magma is called lava. The lava flows out, cools and hardens into igneous rocks of different shapes and patterns.

Red-hot lava oozes slowly from some volcanoes, and spurts out with a fiery explosion from others.

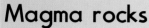

This lava has cooled into long, sausage-like shapes known as pahoehoe, or ropy lava.

Layers of rock

Sedimentary rocks are made from millions
and millions of tiny pieces, or particles,
which have been squeezed together.

Squashed into rock

Over millions of years, wind, rain, rivers and ice wear
away parts of the Earth into tiny pieces, such as sand,
mud and **silt**. These get washed into rivers and are carried
out to sea, where they sink to the bottom in layers known
as **sediments**. As the layers pile up, the lowest ones are
squashed into rocks, such as sandstone and limestone.

Sedimentary layers
on the seabed

Earth's movements
break the layers

Layers of particles on the seabed are
pressed into sedimentary rocks.

The Painted Hills in
Oregon, United States,
were once silt, clay and
mud left when a river
flooded the land.

Changing rocks

Once rocks are formed they can be changed in many ways. Massive movement of the Earth can push them up into mountains. These movements may also press rocks down into the magma. Heat and pressure in deep layers can 'cook' igneous and sedimentary rock types, changing them into rocks called metamorphic rocks. Marble is a metamorphic rock.

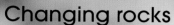

Tell me more!

Rocks from seabed sediments, such as chalk and limestone, often contain the remains of plants and animals. These are called **fossils**. Some types of chalk are mostly made up of fossils!

In millions of years, these mud banks by the River Ganges in India may become hard rock.

19

Caves

Rainwater that seeps deep into the cracks in rocks sometimes creates amazing cave systems.

Cracks and shafts

After it rains, water seeps into the ground through the soil. This rainwater will gradually sink deeper and deeper through cracks in the rock. Sometimes, streams and even small rivers can disappear through vertical shafts called **sinkholes**. The water may reappear again many miles away.

Stalactites form very slowly, drip by drip. They sometimes get so heavy they break off.

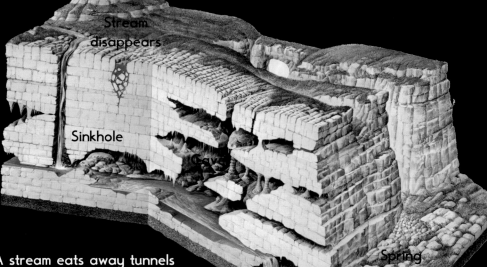

Stream disappears

Sinkhole

Cave

Spring

A stream eats away tunnels and caves in a limestone hill and reappears lower down the slope.

Tell me more!

The world's biggest cave system is Mammoth Cave in Kentucky in the United States. More than 580 kilometres of cave have been found. Despite its name, the remains of **mammoths** have never been found in the cave!

Stalagmites 'grow' about two centimetres every 100 years.

Limestone caves

Most caves form in limestone rock. This is because limestone is slowly eaten away, or dissolved, by rainwater. At first the caves are full of water. As more limestone dissolves, the caves deepen and the higher parts become dry. Water dripping from the roof leaves behind particles of limestone that form icicle-shaped stalactites. Where it drips onto the floor, it can build upside-down versions known as stalagmites.

Earth minerals

Rocks are made of substances
called minerals. Some of these
are very precious and beautiful.

Rare and precious

Minerals form deep in the Earth
over long periods of time. Some,
such as gypsum,
calcite and various
kinds of salt, are
very common.
Others, such as
diamonds and
gold, are rare and
precious. Some
rocks are also
valuable. These
include granite
and marble,
which are used
in buildings.

Pure gold is sometimes found in streams.

Mexico's Cave of
Crystals contains
amazingly shaped
crystals, some more
than 10 metres long.

Digging mines

To take rocks and minerals from the Earth, we dig mines. In a deep-shaft mine, sideways tunnels are made at the bottom of a deep hole. Open-cast mines and quarries, or giant pits, are created near the surface. Rocks and minerals are removed from these by using huge excavator machines and explosives.

Dynamite breaks apart rocks in an open-cast mine.

Amethyst is a form of the mineral quartz.

Tell me more!

Diamonds are made of **carbon** and can take billions of years to form. They are created deep inside the Earth under great heat and pressure. Diamonds only find their way to the Earth's surface when they are carried up by the flow of magma.

23

Fossils

When animals and plants die, their bodies usually rot away. After a few years, there is nothing left. In some cases, however, **traces** of their hard parts remain.

How fossils form

Fossils are found in sedimentary rocks. They are both the preserved hard parts of animals, such as bones, teeth and shells, and the impression or shape of animals left in the mud. Many fossils of the hard parts of plants, such as the bark and seeds, have also been found. The parts are buried in sediments and, like the sediments, they gradually turn into solid rock over millions of years.

Tell me more!

In 2009, fossil hunters in France found the world's biggest dinosaur footprints – each one was about 1.5 metres across! These footprints were probably made by a 30-tonne **sauropod** about 150 million years ago.

Fossils enable scientists to reconstruct the skeletons of ancient creatures.

Fossil record

Fossils tell us about the kinds of animals and plants that lived in the past. This is called the fossil record. It shows how life changed, or evolved, over millions of years. Knowing how fast the layers of sedimentary rocks were laid down allows us to work out the age of the fossils.

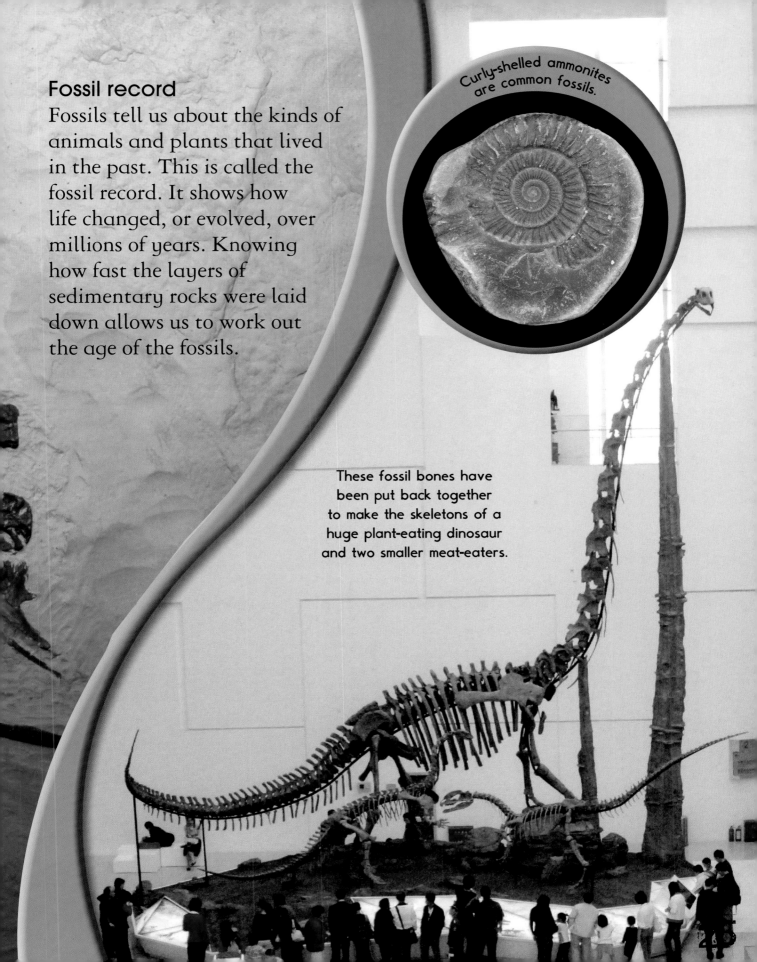

Curly-shelled ammonites are common fossils.

These fossil bones have been put back together to make the skeletons of a huge plant-eating dinosaur and two smaller meat-eaters.

Fossil fuels

Vast amounts of coal are dug from the earth.

The coal, oil and **natural gas** that we use today are known as fossil fuels. They were made millions of years ago from dead plants and animals.

Coal from plants

Hundreds of millions of years ago, giant plants grew in **swamps**. As the plants died, they fell into the water, forming layers. The plants did not rot very fast, and they piled up deeper. Gradually, they were covered by sediments and squashed, forming the black rock called coal.

Oil platform

Oil deposit

Oil rigs drill through the seabed to reach trapped oil and gas.

Oil and natural gas

A long time ago, tiny animals and plants called **plankton** lived in the seas – just as they do today. As they died, they sank and settled in the mud. This muddy layer was then slowly covered over, compressed and became hot. This process turned the squashed material into oil and natural gas. When trapped by a layer of hard rock above, the oil and gas collected, ready to be discovered millions of years later.

Tell me more!

Digging coal out of the ground can be very hard work. But not for the world's biggest digging machine! Trencher 2 is the length of two-and-a-half football pitches end to end!

Oil platforms guide oil or gas along undersea pipelines, or load it into giant tanker ships.

Hot Earth

In some places around the world, hot rocks are found near the surface. We can use their heat to make electricity and to warm ourselves and our homes.

Hot geysers

Heat from the Earth is known as geothermal energy. In some places, such as New Zealand, you can touch the rocks and feel their warmth. Water trickling through deep cracks in the rocks may burst out as a shower of steam and boiling water. This is known as a geyser.

The Pohutu Geyser in New Zealand sprays out scalding water and steam up to 100 metres into the air every 30 minutes.

Once a geothermal power station is built, like this one in Iceland, it costs very little to run. Also, it does not produce greenhouse gases or other forms of pollution.

Geothermal electricity

To make geothermal electricity, holes for pipes are drilled deep into hot rocks. Cold water is then pumped down through one set of pipes and comes up through another set very hot. The heat can be used to generate electricity in a geothermal power station.

Hot springs are popular with Japanese macaque monkeys, who relax in the warm water.

Glossary

Carbon Natural substance that forms coal and diamonds and is found in many kinds of rocks.

Comet Big ball of ice and dust going around the Sun.

Compass Long, slim magnetised needle that points north–south.

Fossil Remains of a living thing preserved in rocks.

Igneous rock Rock formed when melted lava or magma cools and hardens.

Mammoth Huge elephant-like creature which is now extinct (has died out).

Metamorphic rock Rock that is changed by great heat and pressure, but without melting.

Natural gas Gas found in the Earth's crust that we burn as fuel.

Plankton Tiny plants and animals floating in seas and big lakes.

Radioactive substance Substance that gives off rays, which can harm living things.

Sauropod Group of very big dinosaurs with a small head, long neck and tail, huge body and four straight legs.

Sediment Tiny bits or particles that settle into layers.

Sedimentary rock Rock formed by squeezing together particles of sediments.

Silt Very small or fine particles of sediments, like slippery mud.

Sinkhole Deep hole at the surface into which water flows underground.

Supernova A massive exploding star.

Swamp Place with both ground and water, often lots of muddy pools and soft, wet soil.

Trace A sign, or tiny remains of an animal or plant that died long ago.

Index

Ideas for parents and teachers

Here are some practical activities that children can do at school or at home.

Edible Earth

Use a glass tumbler to build up, in layers, a cross-section of the Earth. Make the hard, inner core from toffee and the outer core from jelly. Use a mixture of crispy cereal and marshmallow for the mantle. Make the crust from chocolate, complete with mountains! If hot ingredients are used, children should be supervised.

Create a compass

To make a working compass you will need a sewing needle, a magnet, a small circular piece of cork or plastic and a dish of water.
• Magnetise the needle by stroking it with the magnet in the same direction 30 times.
• Rest the needle on top of the cork and float the cork on the water. Slowly, the needle will turn to point north and south.

Salt crystals

The crystals in a rock such as granite take a long time to form. Salt crystals, however, form very quickly. To make salt crystals you will need 15 ml of hot water, 2.5 ml of table salt and a cup and saucer.
• Stir the salt into the hot water in a cup.
• When the salt has dissolved, pour the liquid into the saucer and leave to cool.
• As the water evaporates over two or three days, the salt crystals will begin to form. The slower the cooling, the bigger the crystals will be.

Chocolate fossils

For this activity you wil need a roll of cooking foil, flat seashells, a small spoon, cooking oil and some chocolate.
• Cover the inside of the clean seashells with cooking foil. Carefully rub the foil down with a small spoon.
• Thinly coat the foil with the oil.
• Pour in some melted cooking chocolate. This stage should be carefully supervised.
• When it has hardened in the shell, take out each chocolate fossil.

Fossils in walls

Look for traces of fossils in the walls of buildings made from limestone. Use thin white paper and crayons to make rubbings of any fossils found. If necessary, seek permission from the owner of the building before starting this activity.

Past and present poems

Write a two-verse poem about the life-story of an animal fossil. As a starting point, you can use the following structure:

First verse: 'Once I was . . .'
Second verse: 'But now I am . . . '

Geology museum

Start collecting rocks, minerals and fossils. Many samples are inexpensive to buy from specialist shops, or can be collected for free. Caution: some sites strictly forbid visitors from collecting samples.